My State OKLAHOMA

By Christina Earley

TABLE OF CONTENTS

A Crabtree Seedlings Book

Crabtree Publishing
crabtreebooks.com

School-to-Home Support for Caregivers and Teachers

This book helps children grow by letting them practice reading. Here are a few guiding questions to help the reader build his or her comprehension skills. Possible answers appear in red.

Before Reading:

- What do I know about Oklahoma?
    - *I know that Oklahoma is a state.*
    - *I know that Oklahoma has plains.*
- What do I want to learn about Oklahoma?
    - *I want to learn which famous people were born in Oklahoma.*
    - *I want to learn what the state flag looks like.*

During Reading:

- What have I learned so far?
    - *I have learned that Oklahoma City is the state capital of Oklahoma.*
    - *I have learned that Oklahoma is one of the states that grows the most wheat in the U.S.*
- I wonder why...
    - *I wonder why the state flower is the Oklahoma rose.*
    - *I wonder why Guthrie is no longer the capital of Oklahoma.*

After Reading:

- What did I learn about Oklahoma?
    - *I have learned that the National Cowboy and Western Heritage Museum has the largest collection of rodeo photographs in the world.*
    - *I have learned that the state animal is the American buffalo.*
- Read the book again and look for the glossary words.
    - *I see the word **capital** on page 5, and the word **pioneer** on page 20. The other glossary words are found on pages 22 and 23.*

OKLAHOMA
Hi! My name is Chet. Welcome to Oklahoma!

I live in Guthrie. There are many **historic** buildings in my city.

My city was the first **capital** of Oklahoma!

Oklahoma is in the south central United States. The capital is Oklahoma City.

Fun Fact: Oklahoma City is the largest city in Oklahoma.

The state animal is the American buffalo.

The Oklahoma rose is the state flower.

We grow a lot of wheat in Oklahoma. Some of it is used to make cereal.

Fun Fact: Oklahoma is one of the states that grows the most wheat in the U.S.

My state flag is blue. It has a **shield** with feathers in the middle.

There is one national sports team in Oklahoma.

My family and I like to visit the National Cowboy and Western Heritage Museum.

Fun Fact: The National Cowboy and Western Heritage Museum has the largest collection of rodeo photographs in the world.

I like to hike to the Black Mesa summit. It is the highest point in Oklahoma.

It is exciting to see bison at the Joseph H. Williams Tallgrass Prairie **Preserve**.

Stephen Hillenburg, the creator of SpongeBob SquarePants, was born in Oklahoma. Singer Carrie Underwood was also born in Oklahoma.

Fun Fact: Sam Walton, the **founder** of Walmart, was born in Kingfisher, Oklahoma.

The Guymon **Pioneer** Days Rodeo is fun to watch!

I like to go fishing at Broken Bow Lake.

Glossary

capital (cap-ih-tuhl): The city or town where the government of a country, state, or province is located

founder (fown-der): A person who creates or starts a business or organization

historic (hi-stor-ik): Something that is important in history

pioneer (pahy-uh-neer): A person who is one of the first to settle and live in a new area

preserve (pri-zurv): An area where animals and plants are protected

shield (sheeld): A piece of metal, wood, or other material that is carried for protection from attack

Index

About the Author

Christina Earley lives in sunny South Florida with her husband and son. She enjoys traveling around the United States and learning about different historical places. Her hobbies include hiking, yoga, and baking.

Written by: Christina Earley

Designed and Illustrated by: Bobbie Houser

Series Development: James Earley

Proofreader: Melissa Boyce

Educational Consultant: Marie Lemke M.Ed.

Photographs:
Alamy: AFF: p. 18 left; ZUMA Press, Inc.: p. 19, 22
Newscom: Melissa Tamez/Icon Sportswire EGV: p. 13
Shutterstock: angie oxley: cover; Patrick Horton: p. 3; RaksyBH: p. 4, 22; Kit Leong: p. 5, 14-15; Volina: p. 6, 22; Sean Pavone: p. 7; O.S. Fisher: p. 8; sokurac: p. 9; Charles Lemar Brown: p. 10-11, 16; oticki: p. 11; railway fx: p. 12, 23; Margo Harrison: p. 15; The Bohemian Lens: p. 17, 23; Kathy Hutchins: p. 18 right; Timothy S. Allen: p. 20, 23; Maclane Parker: p. 21

Crabtree Publishing

crabtreebooks.com 800-387-7650

Printed in the U.S.A./072023/CG20230214

Published in Canada
Crabtree Publishing
616 Welland Avenue
St. Catharines, Ontario
L2M 5V6

Published in the United States
Crabtree Publishing
347 Fifth Avenue
Suite 1402-145
New York, New York, 10016

Library and Archives Canada Cataloguing in Publication
Available at Library and Archives Canada

Library of Congress Cataloging-in-Publication Data
Available at the Library of Congress

Hardcover: 978-1-0398-0530-9
Paperback: 978-1-0398-0562-0
Ebook (pdf): 978-1-0398-0626-9
Epub: 978-1-0398-0594-1